Redefining Negotiation
Innovative Approaches to Conflict Resolution

Abraham H. Ford

Table of Contents

1. Introduction ... 2
2. The Evolution of Negotiation: A Brief History ... 3
    2.1. The Dawn of Negotiation: Primitive Societies ... 3
    2.2. Emerging Civilizations and Negotiation ... 3
    2.3. The Influence of Religion and Philosophy ... 4
    2.4. The Renaissance and Beyond ... 4
    2.5. The Modern Art of Negotiation ... 5
    2.6. Negotiating the Future ... 5
3. Understanding Conflict: The Core of Negotiation ... 7
    3.1. Nature and Types of Conflicts ... 7
    3.2. Theories of Conflict ... 8
    3.3. Conflict Analysis Techniques ... 8
    3.4. Impact of Conflict ... 9
4. Revolutionary Approaches to Conflict Identification ... 11
    4.1. Hidden Conflict: The Underlying Discord ... 11
    4.2. Transforming Perception: Redefining Assumptions ... 12
    4.3. Resolving the Right Conflict ... 12
    4.4. The Role of Active Inquiry in Conflict Identification ... 13
    4.5. From Positions to Interests: Unearthing Underlying Desires ... 13
5. Breaking the Barrier: Emotive Aspects in Negotiation ... 15
    5.1. Emotional Intelligence in Negotiation ... 15
    5.2. Understanding and Identifying Emotions in Negotiation ... 16
    5.3. The Impact of Emotional Reactions on Decision-Making ... 16
    5.4. Emotional Manipulation in Negotiation ... 17
    5.5. Emotion Regulation and Management Techniques ... 17
    5.6. Empathy in Negotiation ... 18
6. The Power of Active Listening in Conflict Resolution ... 19
    6.1. The Essence of Active Listening ... 19

   6.2. Active Listening and its Impact on Conflict Resolution 20
   6.3. Techniques of Active Listening in Conflict Resolution 20
   6.4. The Challenges and Pitfalls of Active Listening 21
   6.5. Conclusion 21
7. Negotiating with Empathy: Fostering Harmonious Interactions .. 23
   7.1. The Essence of Empathic Negotiation 23
   7.2. Fostering Empathy: A Practicable Skill 24
   7.3. Empathy in Action: From Transactional to
   Transformational 24
   7.4. Empathy: The Cornerstone of Harmonious Interactions 25
8. Innovative Strategies: Non-Verbal Communication in
Negotiation 26
   8.1. Decoding the World of Non-Verbal Communication 26
   8.2. The Impact of Non-Verbal Communication in Negotiation ... 27
   8.3. Key Elements of Non-Verbal Communication in Negotiation. 27
   8.4. Practical Examples: Using Non-Verbal Communication in
   Negotiation 28
   8.5. Conclusion: Non-Verbal Communication - A Negotiator's
   Secret Weapon 29
9. The Role of Cultural Intelligence in Effective Negotiation 30
   9.1. The Intricacies of Cultural Intelligence 30
   9.2. Cultural Intelligence in Negotiation 31
   9.3. The Impact of Cultural Intelligence on Negotiation
   Outcomes 32
   9.4. Cultural Intelligence: A Catalyst for Innovative Conflict
   Resolution 32
10. The Future of Negotiation: AI and Virtual Reality 34
   10.1. Exploring the Intersection of AI and Negotiation 34
   10.2. Virtual Reality: A New Frontier in Negotiation 35
   10.3. The Confluence of AI and VR: Transforming Negotiation

  Landscape 36
  10.4. Embracing the Future: Challenges Ahead 36
  10.5. Navigating the New Reality of Negotiation 37
11. Practical Application: Case Studies and Success Stories 38
  11.1. The Tailor Shop: Power of Active Listening 38
  11.2. The TechStartup: Unveiling Non-Verbal Communication . . . 39
  11.3. Non-Profit Organization: A Lesson in Empathy 39
  11.4. Diplomatic Tables: Deploying Cultural Intelligence 40
  11.5. AI Company Negotiation: The Future is Here 40

The most difficult thing in any negotiation, almost, is making sure that you strip it of the emotion and deal with the facts.

— Howard Baker

Chapter 1. Introduction

In an ever-changing world, it is vital to adapt and evolve, even when it comes to an age-old practice like negotiation. Welcome to our Special Report on "Redefining Negotiation: Innovative Approaches to Conflict Resolution." This compelling report unlocks the latest innovative techniques in conflict resolution, giving you the edge in negotiations whether it be in business, politics, or personal relationships. We don't just present theory; our vibrant, real case examples from across different walks of life underline the effectiveness of these innovative approaches. With a cheerful promise of transformative knowledge, this report could be the game-changer you've been waiting for in your conflict resolution strategies. Grab this special report now and embark on a journey of mastering the art of negotiation in a way you've never seen before!

Chapter 2. The Evolution of Negotiation: A Brief History

The realm of negotiation is age-old, seeded deeply in the foundation of human interaction. It is, essentially, our innate need to relate, communicate, and connect that lays the bricks of negotiation in every social facet, be it politics, business, or the personal sphere. But to truly understand the genesis of negotiation and its subsequent evolution, we have to delve into the annals of history, traversing back to early human civilization. As we journey forward in time, the complexities of negotiation will unfold, revealing how it has shaped and been shaped by human expansion.

2.1. The Dawn of Negotiation: Primitive Societies

In early human societies, negotiation was an essential survival skill. The primal humans used negotiation as a means to share resources, establish territories, form alliances, and, in some cases, prevent conflicts. However, this primitive form of negotiation vastly relied on non-verbal communication. Facial expressions, body gestures, and even the intensity of vocalizations played a crucial role in expressing intent. With the gradual development of language and cognitive abilities, negotiation tactics became more sophisticated, paving the way for reasoned dialogue and debate.

2.2. Emerging Civilizations and Negotiation

As civilizations grew and societal structures became more complex, negotiation became an integral part of governance. For instance, in ancient Greece, the democratic system championed open public debates, a unique form of negotiation where the speaker's rhetoric could influence the decision of the assembly. In the Roman Empire, negotiation was the beating heart of the Senate, with every speech a persuasive endeavor aimed to sway fellow senators' votes. These practices reinforced the importance of negotiation within the political arena and set the stage for its future evolution.

2.3. The Influence of Religion and Philosophy

Religion and philosophy played pivotal roles in molding the negotiation techniques of ancient societies. In Eastern philosophies such as Buddhism and Taoism, negotiation took the form of meditative dialogue, rooted in the principles of balance and harmony. In the Middle East, the Islamic tradition of 'Sulh' set norms for negotiation and conflict resolution based on justice, mercy, and forgiveness. The Christian way of brotherly love influenced the manner of discussions, emphasizing peace, compassion, and understanding. These religious and philosophical precepts upheld negotiation as a means of achieving peace and resolution, enriching its process with moral and ethical guidelines.

2.4. The Renaissance and Beyond

The Renaissance period marked a significant leap in the study and practice of negotiation. Intellectuals started to scrutinize and document negotiation tactics, culminating in influential works like Machiavelli's 'The Prince.' Science, reason, and individualism were emphasized, altering the negotiation landscape. Beyond the Renaissance, negotiation started to become formalized, particularly in the realm of diplomacy and international relations. Trade agreements, peace treaties, colonial dialogues—all became domains where negotiation skills were paramount.

2.5. The Modern Art of Negotiation

Coming into the modern era, the development of the business corporation in the 20th century reiterated the importance of negotiation, giving it a more formal structure. It became an integral part of sales, procurement, union dealings, and high-ranking business decisions. Notably, the 1970s saw Harvard University introduce the Win-Win Theory of negotiation, initiating a paradigm shift from adversarial negotiation to collaborative problem-solving. Today, negotiation is hailed as a learnable and essential skill in all corridors of professional leadership. Its essence has permeated beyond boardrooms and political summits, becoming a valuable tool for everyday life and interpersonal relationships.

2.6. Negotiating the Future

As we stand on the threshold of the 21st century, negotiation continues to mold and be molded by evolving societal trends and technological advancements. The rise of artificial intelligence, virtual reality, and digital communication platforms present fresh challenges and opportunities, reshaping the way we negotiate. The future promises a negotiation landscape that's even more dynamic and complex. The only certainty is that negotiation, as a vital component of human interaction, is here to stay.

In this brief historical journey, we can see that negotiation has evolved from primitive interactions to become a complex, structured process governing myriad human engagements. It's been imprinted with ethical principles, diplomatic subtleties, business strategies, and technological progress, signifying its adaptability and relevance across changing eras. As we move forward, this ever-evolving art is being continually redefined, shaped by newer-generation ideals, technological innovations, and global demands, making its mastery an even more compelling requirement. This chapter sets a historical backdrop against which our understanding of the innovative negotiation techniques can be contextually enriched in the subsequent chapters.

Chapter 3. Understanding Conflict: The Core of Negotiation

Understanding conflict closely, in all its intricacies and nuances, forms the cornerstone of our journey into the realms of negotiation. From minor disagreements to heavily strained relationships, conflicts are a part of our daily lives. They may arise in varying scenarios, ranging from boardroom deals to interpersonal issues. Hence, gaining an exploratory understanding of conflict is a critical prerequisite to mastering the art of negotiation.

3.1. Nature and Types of Conflicts

Firstly, let's delve into the nature and different types of conflicts that exist. Essentially, conflict is an inevitable aspect of human interaction. When interests, values, goals or needs clash, a conflict arises. They can be classified into different types based on their causes, parties involved, and the nature of the issues at stake.

1. Interpersonal conflicts: These conflicts originate from disagreements or disputes between two or more individuals. They can be caused by competition, differing personalities, or clashing beliefs.
2. Intra-group conflicts: These conflicts occur within a group. Members in the group may disagree on group goals, individual roles, or task distribution.
3. Inter-group conflicts: These conflicts take place between different groups or teams. They could be due to rivalry, opposing objectives, or incompatible strategies.
4. Organizational conflicts: These are conflicts within an

organization, which may involve employees, management, and the leadership. Reasons can include disagreement on strategic directions, resource allocation, or power dynamics.

Each conflict type requires a distinct approach for effective negotiation and resolution, hence identifying the type is of paramount importance.

3.2. Theories of Conflict

Unpacking the dynamics of conflict, various theories have been proposed over the years to understand its pervasive nature, chiefly among them being Realistic Group Conflict Theory, Social Identity Theory, and Conflict Escalation Theory.

- Realistic Group Conflict Theory posits that competition over scarce resources often induces conflict between groups.
- Social Identity Theory, on the other hand, suggests that people tend to categorize themselves into in-groups and out-groups, thus leading to conflicts between different social identities.
- Conflict Escalation Theory explains how a small disagreement can transform into a major conflict if left unaddressed and is recognized by its distinct five stages - latent conflict, perceived conflict, felt conflict, manifest conflict, and conflict aftermath.

Becoming conversant with these theories offers vital insights into how conflicts emerge, morph, and potentially resolve, thus equipping us with the knowledge to handle them effectively.

3.3. Conflict Analysis Techniques

Armed with an understanding of the nature, types and theories of conflicts, it's crucial that we have the right tools to analyze conflicts. Conflict analysis techniques facilitate negotiation parties to break down the conflict into manageable components and take a fresh look at the problem. There are several conflict analysis techniques, but we will focus on two of the most effective methods: the Conflict Tree Analysis and the Conflict Matrix Analysis.

1. Conflict Tree Analysis: This technique helps identify root causes (represented as roots), core issues or problems (depicted as the trunk) and the effects (represented as branches) of conflict. Oftentimes, negotiators focus on treating the effects of conflict, while the root causes remain unaddressed. Conflict Tree Analysis forces us to consider these underlying factors and tackle the issues more holistically.
2. Conflict Matrix Analysis: Useful in complicated conflicts with multiple issues, parties, and variables. The matrix aids in visualizing the situation, systematically categorizing various elements of the conflict, and understanding complex relationships between them.

Our comprehension of these conflict analysis techniques could provide us an upper hand in the negotiation processes by allowing us to understand and address conflicts at a deeper level.

3.4. Impact of Conflict

Lastly, let's turn our attention to the impact of conflict. The outcomes of conflicts, negative or positive, have profound implications on the individuals and groups involved. On the one hand, unchecked conflicts can breed discontent, result in damaged relationships, loss of productivity, and may even lead to severe cases of violence or war. On the other hand, if handled tactfully, conflicts can lead to positive changes, opening avenues for dialogue, renewed relationships, and strengthened structures.

Recognizing these impacts can aid negotiators in understanding the stakes involved, and in shaping their negotiation strategies that are not just aimed at resolving conflicts, but also mitigating the negative impact and harnessing the potential positive outcomes.

In conclusion, an understanding of conflict forms the essential foundation on which rests the grand edifice of negotiation. By grasping its nature, types, theories, and impacts, and by effectively utilizing conflict analysis techniques, we can navigate through conflicts with confidence, and make strides in becoming competent negotiators. In the following chapters, we will further explore the numerous facets involved in negotiation.

Chapter 4. Revolutionary Approaches to Conflict Identification

In the realm of negotiation, conflict identification is a critical step that lays the cornerstone for resolution. Historically, conflict identification has relied heavily on the direct cues—explicit disagreements, verbal animosity, and opposing interests. Evolution in our understanding of human psyche and communication has brought forth the necessity to revolutionize this traditional approach towards identifying conflicts.

A significant part of this revolutionary approach focuses on understanding the underlying, often hidden, sources of discord that go beyond the obvious. This comprehension shifts our perspective of negotiation from a competition towards scarce resources, to a shared problem-solving venture.

4.1. Hidden Conflict: The Underlying Discord

When we refer to hidden conflicts, we're talking about clashes that lie beneath the surface. These could be buried issues, unvoiced concerns, or even masked grievances caused by past events. These matters, while not clearly stated, can still heavily influence the negotiation process. Thus, it becomes imperative to delve deeper and uncover these hidden layers.

Cognitive psychologists argue that these hidden conflicts often find their roots in cognitive biases and emotional backdrops. Decoding these roots require a significant understanding of cognitive psychology and emotional intelligence. For instance, recognizing that a persistent disagreement might be due to personal biases can be a breakthrough in the negotiation process.

4.2. Transforming Perception: Redefining Assumptions

Often, the parties involved in a negotiation might have preconceived assumptions about the issue at hand, or the people they are negotiating with. These assumptions can shape the perception of the conflict, causing a bias in its identification. In such instances, it's necessary to redefine these assumptions.

A paradigm shift is required that encourages viewing the conflict from multiple perspectives, exploring alternative interpretations, and questioning the validity of personal beliefs. A multi-factored, systemic approach can attribute roots to conflicts from unexpected sources, such as organizational culture or societal norms, which were hitherto ignored or deemed unrelated.

4.3. Resolving the Right Conflict

In the battlefield of negotiation, it is not uncommon to find parties battling the symptoms rather than the disease. Identifying the core conflict rather than treating its symptoms is a vital step towards effective resolution.

For instance, let's consider a scenario where two business departments are in constant disagreement over budget allocations. A traditional approach might identify this as a mere conflict of interests, focusing on compromise or trade-offs. However, an innovative approach might delve deeper to find hidden issues such as lack of communication or accountability, and address those.

4.4. The Role of Active Inquiry in Conflict Identification

Inquiry, as a tool, goes a long way in facilitating effective conflict identification. It encourages dialogue, introspection, and disclosure, all of which are instrumental in digging beneath the surface and uncovering hidden disagreements.

Active inquiry emphasizes not only on asking insightful questions but also focuses on empathetic listening. It aims to create a safe space for open communication, instrumental in breaking the walls of resistance and disclosing buried conflicts.

4.5. From Positions to Interests: Unearthing Underlying Desires

A radical departure from the traditional approach to conflict identification is the shift from positions to interests. A position is the stated demand, while an interest is the underlying desire or need that fuels the position. Identifying and understanding these hidden interests can dramatically enhance the chances of arriving at a mutually beneficial resolution.

To achieve this, parties need to cultivate transparency and encourage dialogue that dives deeper than the stated position. While focusing on interests might surface more conflicts initially, it paves the path for comprehensive resolution that addresses all underlying issues rather than offering superficial solutions.

In conclusion, the search for new-age solutions to our timeless necessity for negotiation leads us to revolutionary approaches in conflict identification. From recognizing hidden conflicts and challenging personal assumptions, to treating the root cause, active inquiry, and focusing on interests rather than positions—the landscape of conflict identification is indeed evolving. This evolutionary stride is a beacon that illuminates our journey towards more effective, empathetic, and holistic negotiation practices.

Chapter 5. Breaking the Barrier: Emotive Aspects in Negotiation

The realm of negotiation extends far beyond words and logic - it delves deep into the world of emotions. This chapter highlights the importance of understanding and managing the emotive aspects that can play a pivotal role in defining the tone and outcome of a negotiation process.

5.1. Emotional Intelligence in Negotiation

Emotional intelligence - the capacity to be aware of, control, and express one's emotions, and to handle interpersonal relationships judiciously and empathetically - is a critical factor in achieving successful negotiation outcomes. Not only does it help negotiators understand their own emotions, but also allows them to recognize and interpret the emotional responses of their counterparts.

The more adept a negotiator becomes at identifying emotions in themselves and others, the better equipped they are to shape their strategies in a way that builds rapport, defuses tension, and mines concessions. Harnessing emotional intelligence involves ways to stay composed under stress, temper aggressiveness with diplomacy, motivate the negotiating partner, and empathize with their perspectives.

5.2. Understanding and Identifying Emotions in Negotiation

Being able to identify emotions at play - both those displayed and those that may be hidden beneath the surface - is a pivotal part of any negotiation. These emotions can often significantly influence the direction and outcome of the negotiation process.

The identification of emotions requires careful attention to the other party's verbal and non-verbal cues, including tone of voice, body language, and facial expressions. Beyond this, recognizing discrepancies between a party's expressed opinions and their actual feelings can shine a light onto deep-seated issues, unmet needs, or potential leverage points.

5.3. The Impact of Emotional Reactions on Decision-Making

Emotions can dramatically sway the course of decision-making in negotiation. Under the influence of strong, impactful emotions - such as anger, fear, or frustration - parties involved may make hurried decisions without taking into account all relevant information. On the other hand, positive emotions like joy, satisfaction, or relief, may enable more open-mindedness and creativity, leading to potentially beneficial compromises or non-traditional solutions. Hence, managing emotional reactions effectively is crucial in the process of negotiation, ensuring decisions are not impulsively harmed by extreme emotions.

5.4. Emotional Manipulation in Negotiation

While an understanding and appreciation of emotions can be used positively to facilitate a win-win negotiation, there's also a darker side to consider. Some negotiators may use emotional manipulation as a tactic to force their own agenda. They may attempt to induce guilt, fear, or anger in their opponent deliberately to cloud their judgement and lead them to give more concessions than they otherwise would. Awareness and recognition of such tactics can assist in the detection and discouragement of such manipulative behavior.

5.5. Emotion Regulation and Management Techniques

Taking control of emotions during negotiation is an essential aspect of managing the negotiation process itself. Emotion regulation refers to the processes by which individuals influence their own feelings and the manner in which they experience and express these emotions.

Techniques for managing emotions during negotiations may involve:

1. Deep breathing exercises and mindfulness techniques to maintain calm.
2. Self-reflection and emotional self-awareness.
3. Focusing on the bigger picture rather than getting embroiled in minor disputes.
4. Mindful communication, ensuring that words and tone are appropriately measured.

Understanding and managing emotional undercurrents can turn the tide in a negotiation, reframing seemingly insurmountable hurdles into opportunities for dialogue, understanding, and compromise. By acknowledging and skillfully handling these emotive aspects, negotiators can build stronger connections and work towards more mutually beneficial outcomes.

5.6. Empathy in Negotiation

Empathy, the ability to understand and share the feelings of others, is a powerful tool in negotiation. An empathetic negotiator can identify the needs, desires, and fears of their opponent, allowing for more effective communication and solution-building. By showing genuine interest in the other party's position and acknowledging their feelings and concerns, a negotiator can foster a climate of trust and mutual respect. This can lead to more productive conversations, and often, collaborative problem-solving.

In conclusion, a negotiation isn't just a discussion of facts, figures, demands, or compromises - it is a complex emotional exchange. Understanding and managing these emotive aspects can not only fuel the trajectory of negotiations but also shape their outcomes in profound and meaningful ways. As negotiators grow more attuned to the emotional ebb and flow of negotiations, they can build more fulfilling, productive, and sustainable relationships, both within and outside the negotiation room.

Chapter 6. The Power of Active Listening in Conflict Resolution

Active listening plays a pivotal role in conflict resolution. Its power lies not only in the ability to express empathy and understanding towards the speaker but also in opening avenues for constructive dialogues, leading to effective conflict resolution. Its fundamental tenets include giving undivided attention to the speaker, comprehending the content and emotions behind the message, responding without judgement, and remembering the information conveyed for future reference.

6.1. The Essence of Active Listening

Active listening is a skill that requires practice and patience. It involves fully dedicating oneself to the act of listening and avoiding any distraction, internal or external. A good listener pays attention to the speaker's words, emotions, body language, tone, and the overall context in which the conversation is taking place. It is not limited merely to hearing; it includes understanding and interpreting the speaker's message.

Active listening requires immediate feedback, which distinguishes it from passive listening. Feedback is offered through verbal affirmations, body language that demonstrates engagement, or recapitulation of the speaker's key points to ensure understanding. Active listeners are always prepared to ask questions, which allow them to better absorb the message and signal the speaker their interest in what is being said.

6.2. Active Listening and its Impact on Conflict Resolution

When it comes to conflict resolution, active listening can serve as a powerful tool. Conflicts often arise from miscommunication which could be mitigated by effective active listening. It encourages parties to better articulate their viewpoints, concerns, and feelings, fostering a sense of respect and validation. It facilitates problem-solving by preventing misunderstandings and promoting cooperative dialogue.

Active listening aids in reducing negative emotions tied with conflicts - anxiety, hostility, defensiveness, and frustration. When someone realizes they are genuinely listened to and their viewpoints are respected, they are more likely to reciprocate the same behavior. It creates an atmosphere of mutual understanding and empathy, which is essential for resolving conflicts.

6.3. Techniques of Active Listening in Conflict Resolution

Effective active listening in conflict resolution necessitates the adoption of several techniques.

Paraphrasing: A summary or rephrasing of the speaker's words, affirming that the listener is following along. Paraphrasing not only validates the speaker, but also allows the listener to confirm their understanding of the message.

Reflecting: Involves repeating back the speaker's emotional state or feelings. This technique demonstrates an understanding of the speaker's emotions, contributing to a deeper connection and rapport-building.

Clarifying: Asking questions to understand better or seeking further information. Clarifying questions eliminate assumptions, helping in averting misunderstandings.

Non-Verbal Cues: Utilizing body language to show engagement, such as maintaining eye contact, nodding, or leaning forward. Non-verbal cues can express attentiveness and genuine interest in the conversation.

Validating: Acknowledging the speaker's viewpoints and feelings without necessarily agreeing with them. Validation affirms the worth of the speaker's experience.

6.4. The Challenges and Pitfalls of Active Listening

While active listening creates a foundation for effective conflict resolution, mastering it is not without challenges. It requires emotional intelligence, patience, authentic interest, and self-restraint. The listener must abstain from interrupting the speaker, refrain from making assumptions or prematurely formulating responses.

Fallacies or misconceptions about active listening can also impede its effectiveness. For instance, some might erroneously equate active listening with agreement, leading them to avoid it when they disagree with the speaker. However, active listening simply involves understanding the speaker's perspective, not necessarily endorsing it. Overcoming such misconceptions is integral to harnessing the power of active listening in conflict resolution.

6.5. Conclusion

In conclusion, the power of active listening in conflict resolution cannot be overstated. It brings forth understanding, empathy, respect, and validation, all of which are crucial for resolving conflicts. By honing this skill, one can promote healthier, more constructive interactions, not only in conflicts but in all realms of communication.

Chapter 7. Negotiating with Empathy: Fostering Harmonious Interactions

In navigating through the labyrinth of human interactions, empathy emerges as an unparalleled tool, an unexpected hero in the realm of negotiation. The ability to understand and share the feelings of others is not merely a conversational nicety; instead, it's a profound approach to conflict resolution and, therefore, an indispensable negotiation tactic. This chapter dissects the significance of empathy in negotiation, exploring how to cultivate and apply it for more fruitful, harmonious interactions.

7.1. The Essence of Empathic Negotiation

Empathic negotiation is a far cry from the stereotypical image of negotiators we often envisage as relentless, firm, and at times, confrontational individuals. In contrast, empathic negotiation exhorts understanding, communication, and conciliation. It involves understanding the other party's emotions, concerns, and perspectives-a skill that necessitates patience, composure, and the ability to listen actively. It's not about winning a duel but building a bridge that connects two sides.

An essential aspect of empathic negotiation is mirroring-the process of reflecting the other party's emotions, attitudes, and speech patterns. This sends a strong, non-verbal message that you empathize with their point of view and facilitates a sense of unity. Simultaneously, it discourages defensive behaviors which may emerge out of feeling misunderstood or undervalued, helping to keep the negotiation conversation congenial.

7.2. Fostering Empathy: A Practicable Skill

Empathy isn't an inborn trait; it is eminently learnable. Several practices can help foster empathy, a few of which include curious questioning, active listening, and perspective-taking. These aren't merely rhetorical tools but powerful strategies that can redefine your position in a negotiation scenario.

Curious questioning involves asking open-ended questions to understand the other party's thoughts, feelings, and motivations better. Conversely, active listening entails understanding their message without getting sidetracked by the task of formulating responses. Finally, perspective-taking involves placing oneself in the other person's shoes, fostering a more profound understanding of their viewpoint. All these techniques work together to enhance your empathic negotiation capabilities.

7.3. Empathy in Action: From Transactional to Transformational

By developing empathic negotiation skills such as curious questioning, active listening, and perspective-taking, you can transition from transactional negotiations to transformational ones. In transactional negotiation, the goal is exchanging items of comparable value, where parties engage in hard bargaining. In contrast, transformational negotiation allows the parties to understand each other's needs, creating opportunities for widespread benefits and win-win solutions.

Empathic negotiation fosters this transformational change by subverting traditional power dynamics and competition. By seeking to understand before being understood, you encourage collaboration, open dialogue, and mutual benefit. This kinder, empathic approach is not a means to manipulate; instead, it's about approaching negotiation with a humanistic perspective, making the process more about mutual understanding than about winning or losing.

7.4. Empathy: The Cornerstone of Harmonious Interactions

Empathy's transformative power can convert antagonistic interactions into collaborative dialogues. By embracing empathy, negotiators can provoke a paradigm shift within the realm of conflict resolution. This shift harbors the chance to redefine negotiation norms, encouraging cooperation, long-term relationships, and mutual success.

Skilled empathy enables negotiators to address sensitive issues tactfully, fostering psychological safety—the assurance that it's safe for others to express their thoughts and feelings. Thus, empathy plays a pivotal role in building trust, cooperation, and understanding, leading to more harmonious and successful interactions.

In conclusion, empathy, often overlooked in negotiation, present an operative framework for fostering harmonious interactions. As we grow to appreciate empathy's value within negotiations, we see the birth of a new standard-negotiation not as a war to be won, but as a dance of understanding, respect, and mutual benefit. Through curious questioning, active listening, and perspective-taking, negotiators can wield the power of empathy, fostering a bond far mightier than the crude force of a one-sided victory—the bond of shared humanity and understanding, laced with trust and sustainable resolutions.

Chapter 8. Innovative Strategies: Non-Verbal Communication in Negotiation

In the vast landscape of human interaction, there is a silent ocean where words are mere currents. It is within this ocean that 93% of our communication transpires. This, dear reader, is the world of non-verbal communication.

8.1. Decoding the World of Non-Verbal Communication

Non-verbal communication is a phenomenon that silently commands our social and professional lives. It forms the less obvious sphere of our communication, buried deep beneath the written or spoken word. This includes facial expressions, postures, gestures, eye contact, spatial arrangements, patterns of touch, expressive movement, cultural habits, and other 'silent' cues that play a pivotal role in shaping human interaction. These aspects shape the perception of your sincerity, credibility, and reliability in negotiations, without even a word being spoken.

To master the art of negotiation, it's crucial to understand, decode, and use non-verbal cues effectively. This is why understanding the language of non-verbal communication becomes a game-changer in negotiations. Imagine an iceberg. The small portion above the water represents the verbal communication we engage in during negotiations, while the enormous part submerged underwater signifies the non-verbal communication shaping the negotiation's overall undercurrents.

8.2. The Impact of Non-Verbal Communication in Negotiation

Every negotiation is as much a perceptual event as it is a substantive exchange of information, ideas, and proposals. To truly gain an edge in negotiations, it's beneficial to understand the power of non-verbal communication. It can be particularly influential because it is more honest – people often have more control over their words than their non-verbal communication. Non-verbal cues can yield valuable insights into the other person's feelings, attitudes, and reactions. Hence, they provide a window into the subconscious mind, revealing truths otherwise concealed by controlled verbal interaction.

Successful negotiators don't just listen with their ears but also with their eyes. They watch for changes in facial expressions, nuances of posture, and shifts in eye contact. These subtle signs can indicate whether the negotiating party is genuinely agreeable to a proposition or merely agreeing on the surface.

8.3. Key Elements of Non-Verbal Communication in Negotiation

Let's delve into dissecting and understanding the individual constituents of non-verbal communication:

- **Posture:** A relaxed and open posture often indicates self-confidence, acceptance, and openness to dialogue. On the contrary, closed postures, such as crossed arms, are usually associated with defensiveness or disagreement.
- **Facial Expressions:** They are perhaps the most straightforward yet nuanced forms of non-verbal communication. They can reveal joy, sadness, anger, surprise, fear, and disgust. Paying close attention to the other party's facial expressions can provide

valuable insight into their emotional state and reactions to propositions.

- **Eye Contact:** Another essential component of non-verbal communication is maintaining eye contact. Sustained, relaxed eye contact indicates honesty, interest, and engagement, while shifty eye movements can suggest discomfort or untruthfulness.
- **Gestures:** While these can vary greatly from culture to culture, certain common gestures convey universal meanings. Hand and arm movements can often reveal a person's level of enthusiasm, willingness to cooperate, frustration, or even deception.
- **Physical distance:** The spatial distance kept between communicators conveys different meanings across cultures. Understanding and respecting each other's comfort zones in terms of physical space can greatly enhance the success of negotiations.

8.4. Practical Examples: Using Non-Verbal Communication in Negotiation

Let's consider a real-life scenario to elucidate these concepts further. In a business negotiation, one party member, Alfred, maintains direct eye contact while conversing, nods affirmatively at engaging points, leans forward to display interest, and exhibits an overall open posture. His smiles are genuine, matching the enthusiastic tone of his speech, his gestures lively but not aggressive. These non-verbal cues transmit a message of engagement, trust, openness, and willingness to engage in a meaningful negotiation.

On the flip side, if Alfred were to maintain minimal eye contact, sit with a closed posture (e.g., arms crossed), give away forced smiles, or display restless fingers, his verbal communication would lose its effect due to contradicting non-verbal cues.

In yet another scenario, a negotiator from a culture where direct eye contact is construed as intrusive or disrespectful could misconstrue Alfred's direct gaze as aggressive. Misinterpretation of such cultural nuances, in the realm of non-verbal communication, could adversely affect the negotiation process.

For effective negotiations, it becomes essential for Alfred, or any negotiator, to not only be mindful of his own range of non-verbal cues but also successfully interpret those from the other party, taking into consideration their behavioral and cultural contexts.

8.5. Conclusion: Non-Verbal Communication - A Negotiator's Secret Weapon

To sum up, the mastery of non-verbal communication can provide an additional edge in any negotiation. By harnessing the power of non-verbal cues, we can accurately deduce the feelings and intentions of opposite parties, even when they remain unexpressed verbally. Furthermore, by being cognizant of our non-verbal messages, we can control and direct negotiations more effectively. It's a silent yet potent weapon in the arsenal of any successful negotiator. Remember, it's not just what you say, but how you say it, how you present it, and how you embody it - that makes all the difference in the world of negotiations.

Chapter 9. The Role of Cultural Intelligence in Effective Negotiation

Emerging as a prevailing force in today's interconnected world, cultural intelligence, often referred to as CQ, has infiltrated the intricate realm of negotiations. The substantial role it plays as a vital cog propelling successful conflict resolution cannot be overstated. In essence, cultural intelligence serves as a potent bridge between diverse cultures, propagating mutual understanding and respect.

9.1. The Intricacies of Cultural Intelligence

Cultural intelligence necessitates a profound understanding of varied cultural nuances, not merely as entity-bound characteristics, but rather as intricate systems influencing behavior, perceptions, and practices. Comprising a blend of cognitive, motivational, and behavioral components, cultural intelligence involves the ability to discern, perceive, and appropriately respond to cultural distinctiveness. It necessitates effectively operating in contexts characterized by cultural diversity, a critical aspect in conflict resolution and negotiation.

Cognitive CQ involves the acquisition of knowledge about cultural norms, practices, and conventions unique to specific cultures. It encapsulates the understanding of cultural similarities and differences along with an aptitude to comprehend multifarious cultural perspectives.

Motivational CQ denotes the intrinsic drive to understand and effectively interact with individuals originating from diverse cultural backgrounds. It's characterized by the curiosity to explore unique cultural dynamics, thus driving a negotiator's readiness to adapt to various cultural apprehensions.

Behavioral CQ, on the other hand, is the aptitude to exhibit suitable verbal and non-verbal behavior in diverse cultural contexts. It underlines the importance of respecting cultural norms, demonstrating situational flexibility, and adapting communication strategies to suit culturally distinctive interactions.

9.2. Cultural Intelligence in Negotiation

In negotiation scenarios, cultural intelligence serves a pivotal role in bridging communication gaps and facilitating constructive dialogue. Not only does it foster open, transparent exchange of ideas, it also ramps up the probability of robust agreements by promoting mutual understanding and aiding in overcoming cultural barriers.

With the insight gleaned by cognitive CQ, a negotiator acquires an unprecedented understanding of the opposite party's cultural norms and key points of divergence. This knowledge steers the negotiator's strategy, enabling the prevention or swift resolution of conflicts that might stem from cultural discrepancies.

Motivational CQ's intricate interplay bolsters negotiations by driving negotiators' intrinsic motivation to connect with diverse individuals. When negotiators are driven to understand, they prove more willing to compromise, fostering an environment conducive to negotiation.

Behavioral CQ shores up negotiation skills by promoting cultural congruence in behavior. This cultural congruence eases perceived or actual tensions and prompts greater patience, avoidance of assumptions, and empathy.

9.3. The Impact of Cultural Intelligence on Negotiation Outcomes

In negotiations, the compelling impact of cultural intelligence can oftentimes spell the difference between deadlock and mutual agreement. It aids in breaking down preconceived notions and biases, paving the way toward amicable resolution. It also heightens awareness of potential cultural breakpoints, thus enabling parties to tread causatively in areas of sensitivity.

Culturally intelligent negotiators tap into their cognitive, motivational, and behavioral intelligence to navigate through the resolution process. By wielding an array of culturally flexible strategies, these negotiators are able to mold their approach to meet the complex demands dictated by diverse cultural backgrounds.

Moreover, research increasingly substantiates the correlation between high levels of cultural intelligence and the success of negotiation outcomes. Culturally intelligent negotiators exhibit greater problem-solving capacity, are adept at preventing or resolving misunderstandings swiftly, and tend to form more durable and robust agreements.

9.4. Cultural Intelligence: A Catalyst for Innovative Conflict Resolution

From this elucidation, it appears undeniable that cultural intelligence, with its multifaceted dimensions, stands as a potent tool for modern negotiation. As the world continues to interweave, fueled by globalization and tech-enabled communication, the role of CQ in peaceful conflict resolution will likely only intensify. By fostering inclusivity, empathy, and mutual understanding, cultural intelligence empowers negotiators to move beyond mere transactions and into the realm of transformational cross-cultural negotiation. Armed with the insights highlighted in this elucidation, we can all become more culturally intelligent and effective negotiators. After all, a successful negotiation isn't merely a win-win outcome; it's a synergistic interaction that fosters cultural appreciation, respect, and mutual growth.

Chapter 10. The Future of Negotiation: AI and Virtual Reality

The advent of rapid technological advancements has continued to push boundaries, influencing every aspect of our lives, including the powerful realm of negotiation. The next frontier seems even more audacious, audacious enough to herald an era where AI and Virtual Reality take center stage. Though it might sound like a trope taken from science fiction, it is quickly becoming an accessible reality.

10.1. Exploring the Intersection of AI and Negotiation

Though still in its infancy, Artificial Intelligence (AI) has found its footprints in an expansive range of applications, from recommendation systems to self-driving cars, and now, negotiation. AI, with its infinite mathematical prowess and gnawing hunger for data, provides us with a tool that can both learn from and mimic human behavior with amazing accuracy. This capability naturally extends into negotiation, which, at its core, is a complex human behavior.

Applications of AI in negotiation can take several forms, from decision support tools equipped with advanced predictive analysis to autonomous programs conducting negotiations on our behalf. For instance, bots might run simulations for thousands of negotiations in a fraction of time, where a decision tree's every branch represents a different negotiation path, helping us determine the most effective strategies. These simulations, powered by machine learning algorithms, are capable of testing different approaches, learning, and refining strategies over time, based on feedback.

AI could also be leveraged to enhance pre-negotiation preparation. By digesting enormous data sets, AI can predict counterparties' behavior, enabling better strategy development. It can even analyse communication patterns for emotional undertones, providing unique insights that may set the negotiation's tenor for success. Nevertheless, embracing AI in negotiation doesn't come without its caveats. We must bear in mind the ethical quandaries and issues related to transparency, trust, and data privacy.

10.2. Virtual Reality: A New Frontier in Negotiation

Looking beyond the confines of traditional negotiation settings, Virtual Reality (VR) provides a ground-breaking environment that can bring a whole new level of immersion and flexibility. Imagine preparing for a negotiation strategy by immersing yourself in a VR environment that mimics the actual negotiation setting. By creating realistic negotiation simulations, VR can help reshape our perception, alter our emotional states, and foster empathy.

In-context training via VR can offer tailored experiences with myriad possible negotiation scenarios. These VR environments can adapt in real-time to your behavior, responses, and negotiation style. Besides, with VR, geographical barriers become irrelevant. You can negotiate in real-time with a counterpart seated across the globe, creating a 'presence.' Such technology can be particularly useful in cross-cultural negotiations, mitigating misunderstanding risks and fostering stronger connections.

10.3. The Confluence of AI and VR: Transforming Negotiation Landscape

The blend of AI and VR can yield something genuinely transformative for the negotiation landscape. The synergy created by AI's analytical intelligence and VR's immersive experience can offer a new dimension to negotiation training and execution. For instance, AI-backed VR simulations can provide real-time feedback, all the while learning from and adapting to the user's actions. This granular, dynamic feedback would revolutionize how we hone our negotiation skills.

Meanwhile, AI can enhance VR negotiations by offering data-driven insights. Picture negotiating with a virtual partner created by AI, who adjusts their behavior in real-time based on your emotional states, identified through your tone of voice, body language, and facial expressions. This level of interactive learning could boost our negotiation proficiency to unprecedented heights.

10.4. Embracing the Future: Challenges Ahead

Notwithstanding the enticing possibilities, the fusion of AI and VR in negotiation also poses significant challenges. The foremost is the ethical conundrum. While AI can provide insightful data, it also raises questions around trust, transparency, and privacy, given the sensitivity of the information involved in negotiations. Additionally, there's a risk of depersonalization in VR negotiations. Maintaining the human touch amidst such digital interface forms a crucial challenge.

Furthermore, technological advancements often outpace regulatory frameworks. To fully unlock the potential of AI and VR in negotiation, we need to ensure they are developed and used responsibly. This necessitates clear regulatory guidelines and ethical standards to engender trust and transparency in these technologies while safeguarding users' interests.

10.5. Navigating the New Reality of Negotiation

As we delve into the new reality where AI and Virtual Reality will likely be significant players in negotiation, we must navigate this emerging landscape wisely. Yet it's essential to remember that while these technologies hold promise, the human connection remains at the heart of negotiations. These technologies should be seen as tools that enhance our ability to communicate and empathize, not replace them.

In this thrilling technological ride into the future of negotiation, caution must be our constant companion. But with open minds and the resilience to adapt, we can leverage the compelling possibilities of AI and VR, transforming negotiation styles and strategies in ways previously unthinkable. This journey won't be effortless or without its challenges, but the destination could well be a new epoch of negotiation proficiency and resolution potentials that transform our world.

Chapter 11. Practical Application: Case Studies and Success Stories

The adage that actions speak louder than words holds a particularly strong resonance here, as we delve into the world of real-world applications - both successes and failures - of the innovative negotiation strategies discussed in previous chapters. Throughout this chapter, we will inspect a range of real-life case studies, from small businesses to multinational corporations, political negotiations to relationship dynamics. Each case serves as a testament to the pioneering theories we've explored, illuminating the varied landscapes in which these strategies find utilisation and transformational impacts. Let's plunge in.

11.1. The Tailor Shop: Power of Active Listening

The first case originates from a humble tailor shop, where a substantial conflict erupted between the owner and an irate customer over a botched bridal gown. The owner, equipped with the power of active listening, deployed his skills to understand the customer's emotional state in conjunction with the practical issue at hand. Noted interruptions were minimal, questions were insightful and reflective, rendering the conversation productive. This stance allowed him to empathise with the bride's predicament, evading defensiveness, and creating space for resolution. The result was a satisfied customer, who instead of leaving a negative review, praised the shop for its excellent customer service.

Here, we witness a straightforward instance of the efficacy of active listening under stress. Instead of becoming confrontational, which can escalate matters, the approach taken was to truly understand and respond. This case underscores the feasibility of applying effective listening techniques to transform potential crises into opportunities for building stronger relationships.

11.2. The TechStartup: Unveiling Non-Verbal Communication

Our second case is a burgeoning tech startup experiencing internal conflict among team members. The discord was primarily attributable to misunderstandings and miscommunication. The CEO, understanding the vital role of non-verbal communication in negotiation, began implementing specific strategies. Training sessions were held featuring exercises on interpreting body language, understanding facial cues, and establishing positive non-verbal communication.

In time, team meetings became decidedly less tense. The team, now having an enhanced understanding of non-verbal cues, was better equipped to navigate conference room dynamics. Theary engagement increased, and the overall productivity rose significantly. Hence, it's evident how an understanding of non-verbal dimensions of communication can radically improve team dynamics.

11.3. Non-Profit Organization: A Lesson in Empathy

The third case is a nationally acclaimed non-profit organization grappling with strained relationships with its donors. An innovative solution was proposed - repositioning their negotiation strategies by placing empathy at the forefront. By applying empathic negotiation tactics, the organization was able to comprehend the priorities, apprehensions, and motivations of their donors better. This tactic proved instrumental in renewing contracts and even securing higher donation amounts.

This practical manifestation of empathy in negotiation exemplifies its potential in fostering robust, long-lasting relationships. Empathic communication created an atmosphere of mutual respect and understanding, ensuring both parties felt valued and heard.

11.4. Diplomatic Tables: Deploying Cultural Intelligence

The effectiveness of cultural intelligence manifests eloquently in political and diplomatic negotiations. A case in point is the Iran nuclear deal, where negotiations involved parties from varied cultural backgrounds. The negotiators' cultural intelligence ensured they respected diverse perspectives and behavioural norms that are integral to different societies. Despite the varied cultural nuances, a deal was struck, testifying how acknowledging and leveraging cultural intelligence can bridge gaps in international negotiations.

11.5. AI Company Negotiation: The Future is Here

Finally, we look at a negotiation powered by advanced technology. An AI company demonstrated its AI negotiation bot, trained on negotiation books, human dialogues, and trained negotiation experts' feedback. Their bot outperformed humans during negotiations in a virtual environment during its latest showcase. Arduous negotiations reduced in complexity and the time considerably shrunk owing to machine speed and efficiency.

Each case in this diverse compilation exhibits how these innovative negotiation strategies pave the way for sustainable solutions. They testify to the transformative effect a mindset shift can bring, fostering relationships and building bridges where once there were walls. In conclusion, redefining negotiation is not just about understanding new methodologies, but it's about how effectively we implement these principles. These success stories encapsulate the essence of innovative negotiation, calling for everyone to embrace and explore these modern approaches in their unique contexts.

www.ingramcontent.com/pod-product-compliance
Lightning Source LLC
Chambersburg PA
CBHW070951220526
45471CB00007B/2981